Published by Angelis Publications
ISBN: 978-0-9956949-6-5
www.angelispublications.com
Cover Design Angie J Anderson
© Angelis Publications 2017

A Celebration of the Life of

"That we once enjoyed and deeply loved we can never lose, for all that we love deeply becomes part of us."

Helen Keller

Name & Address

Thoughts & Memories

Name & Address

Thoughts & Memories

Name & Address

Thoughts & Memories

Name & Address

Thoughts & Memories

Name & Address

Thoughts & Memories

Name & Address

Thoughts & Memories

Name & Address

Thoughts & Memories

Name & Address

Thoughts & Memories

Name & Address

Thoughts & Memories

Name & Address

Thoughts & Memories

Name & Address

Thoughts & Memories

Name & Address

Thoughts & Memories

Name & Address

Thoughts & Memories

Name & Address

Thoughts & Memories

Name & Address

Thoughts & Memories

Name & Address

Thoughts & Memories

Name & Address

Thoughts & Memories

Name & Address

Thoughts & Memories

Name & Address

Thoughts & Memories

Name & Address

Thoughts & Memories

Name & Address

Thoughts & Memories

Name & Address

Thoughts & Memories

Name & Address

Thoughts & Memories

Name & Address

Thoughts & Memories

Name & Address

Thoughts & Memories

Name & Address

Thoughts & Memories

Name & Address

Thoughts & Memories

Name & Address

Thoughts & Memories

Name & Address

Thoughts & Memories

Name & Address

Thoughts & Memories

Name & Address

Thoughts & Memories

Name & Address

Thoughts & Memories

Name & Address

Thoughts & Memories

Name & Address

Thoughts & Memories

Name & Address

Thoughts & Memories

Name & Address

Thoughts & Memories

Name & Address

Thoughts & Memories

Name & Address

Thoughts & Memories

Name & Address

Thoughts & Memories

Name & Address

Thoughts & Memories

Name & Address

Thoughts & Memories

Name & Address

Thoughts & Memories

Name & Address

Thoughts & Memories

Name & Address

Thoughts & Memories

Name & Address

Thoughts & Memories

Name & Address

Thoughts & Memories

Name & Address

Thoughts & Memories

Name & Address

Thoughts & Memories

Name & Address

Thoughts & Memories

Name & Address

Thoughts & Memories

Name & Address

Thoughts & Memories

Name & Address

Thoughts & Memories

Name & Address

Thoughts & Memories

Name & Address

Thoughts & Memories

Name & Address

Thoughts & Memories

Name & Address

Thoughts & Memories

Name & Address

Thoughts & Memories

Name & Address

Thoughts & Memories

Name & Address

Thoughts & Memories

Name & Address

Thoughts & Memories

Name & Address

Thoughts & Memories

Name & Address

Thoughts & Memories

Name & Address

Thoughts & Memories

Name & Address

Thoughts & Memories

Name & Address

Thoughts & Memories

Name & Address

Thoughts & Memories

Name & Address

Thoughts & Memories

Name & Address

Thoughts & Memories

Name & Address

Thoughts & Memories

Name & Address

Thoughts & Memories

Name & Address

Thoughts & Memories

Name & Address

Thoughts & Memories

Name & Address

Thoughts & Memories

Name & Address

Thoughts & Memories

Name & Address

Thoughts & Memories

Name & Address

Thoughts & Memories

Name & Address

Thoughts & Memories

Name & Address

Thoughts & Memories

Name & Address

Thoughts & Memories

Name & Address

Thoughts & Memories

Name & Address

Thoughts & Memories

Name & Address

Thoughts & Memories

Name & Address

Thoughts & Memories

Name & Address

Thoughts & Memories

Name & Address

Thoughts & Memories

Name & Address

Thoughts & Memories

Name & Address

Thoughts & Memories

Name & Address

Thoughts & Memories

Name & Address

Thoughts & Memories

Name & Address

Thoughts & Memories

Name & Address

Thoughts & Memories

Name & Address

Thoughts & Memories

Name & Address

Thoughts & Memories

Name & Address

Thoughts & Memories

CPSIA information can be obtained
at www.ICGtesting.com
Printed in the USA
LVHW062325100422
715849LV00006B/60